QUILA LIME SHRIMP ﹖ CHILI CON TRES VERD﹖

P AND ROLL ﹖ **CAESAR'S UNCLE** ﹖ HOT BIRD ON A BED OF SLA

'S BOYHOOD BEST ﹖ COOKIE'S QUICK COQ AU VIN ﹖ TARTIN

ASH ﹖ **FIRECRACKER SAUCE** ﹖ ONE COLD FISH 2 SAUCES ﹖ P

TY FETA SHRIMP ﹖ **SUPER SOUR CITRUS COOLER** ﹖ ENDLESS T

A PERFECT 3 TIMES ﹖ BEIJING MEETS BROOKLYN ﹖ BOYHOOD

CHEESECAKE ﹖ INSTANT TARTLETS ﹖ **FAJITA CHOP** ﹖ INFINITE

STED SMASHED POTATOES ﹖ PERFECT PEAR IN PARIS ﹖ 3 CO

A CHOP ﹖ **PIZZA PARADE** ﹖ NAKED RIBS ﹖ **DEEP DARK BUMP**

﹖ PULLED BREAD WITH CONFETTI BUTTER ﹖ TEQUILA LIME S

CHEZ MOI ﹖ GREEN WITH ENVY ﹖ BILLY'S BOYHOOD BEST ﹖ E

QUILA LIME SHRIMP ﹖ **HEIRLOOM TOMATO CELEBRATION** ﹖ CHO

HULA SKIRT ﹖ CAESAR'S UNCLE ﹖ TARTINE CHEZ MOI ﹖ INS

PACCIO SANDWICH ﹖ INFINITE ASPARAGUS ﹖ **BUMPY BARK** ﹖

SA ﹖ FIRECRACKER SAUCE ﹖ HOT TOMATO TART ﹖ CITRUS AN

BED OF SLAW ﹖ ENDLESS TOPTIONS CHEESECAKE ﹖ **BRIES W**

PLATE ﹖ **INFINITE ASPARAGUS** ﹖ BILLY'S BOYHOOD BEST ﹖ B

JILA LIME SHRIMP ﹖ CHILI CON TRES VERDES ﹖ **CHOP AND R**

TER & LEMONAISE ﹖ CAESAR'S UNCLE ﹖ FAJITA CHOP ﹖ INST

RIED FRUIT ﹖ **CITRUS SOY SPLASH** ﹖ CREAM CHEESE IN A HU

69 QUICKiES
IN THE KiTCHEN

THE SHOPPING CART CHEF'S
AMAZiNG ASSEMBLIES
FROM **PREPARED FOODS, FRESH PRODUCE,**
THE **SALAD BAR** AND **OFF THE SHELF PRODUCTS.**

by Joan Vogel

PHOTOGRAPHS: JON EDWARDS
FOOD STYLING: NORMAN STEWART
BOOK DESIGN: JON LICHT
FOOD CONSULTANT: KIM CHAN

To Bob + Beverly – your support for all these / for all their years in allll my zany endeavors. Happy V'day – Have fun with your food! Joan Vogel

PUBLISHED BY SHOPPING CART PRESS 2010
SHOPPING CART PRESS, 149 S. BARRINGTON AVE, SUITE 462,
LOS ANGELES, CALIFORNIA 90049 • WWW.69QUICKIESINTHEKITCHEN.COM

ISBN: 978-1-60725-071-5
LIBRARY OF CONGRESS CONTROL NUMBER: 2009910622

PRINTED IN CHINA BY BEACONSTAR

TO BILLY

MY **HUSBAND** AND **PARTNER IN LIFE**
FOR HIS **AMAZING LOVE** AND **PATIENCE** WITH THIS PROJECT.

HE NEVER LET ME GIVE UP ON MY CRAZY DREAM OF
'QUICKIES IN THE KITCHEN.'

I COULD NEVER HAVE DONE IT WITHOUT HIM.

3 min

5 min

5 min

WHAT'S
IN
YOUR
BAG?

NAVIGATING THE AISLES
WITH THE SHOPPING CART CHEF

*We have used specific brands in some of our assemblies.
For more information refer to the 'Brands We Love' section.

**APPROACH
L♥VE
& COOKING
WiTH RECKLESS ABANDON**

Dalai Lama

INTRODUCTION to

69 QUICKIES IN THE KITCHEN. A LOOSE AND LANKY NO-COOK-COOKBOOK.

almost

This book is for people who enjoy great food but have no time. The key is knowing what to put in your shopping cart.

'**Quickies**' has no conventional recipes; just assemblies; some more casual than others. They all combine fresh prepared with ready made and easy assembly.

Every department and shelf in today's markets is full of staggering options. Taking advantage of these convenient resources isn't cheating, it's just plain smart. Think of your supermarket as your **secret sous-chef** and **one stop partner** in the kitchen.

HOW ABOUT?

-Asking the Prepared Foods staff to give you 2 **rotisserie chickens**, *no salt, please. Buy a pound of ready-roasted* **potatoes**.

-Have the Fresh Seafood Department poach a salmon, or cook and clean a lobster.

-Get some **wild rice salad** *from the Salad Bar...toss it with* **Briannas' Ginger Mandarin Dressing**.

-Don't forget a jar of **green salsa**. **Stone ground mustard** *is a must.* **Ojai Cook 'Lem-onaise'** *ALWAYS comes in handy.*

-Throw some fresh **pestos** *and* **pastas** *into your cart along with a couple of exotic* **cheeses** *as you pass the refrigerated section.*

-Defrost a **cheesecake** *and scatter some fresh* **berries** *on top.*

There are so many choices and around every corner there is **another quickie**. **GIVE YOURSELF SOME WIGGLE ROOM**, **CREATE SOMETHING DIFFERENT** and **HAVE FUN**.

Come with me on a zany and wonderful culinary journey up and down the aisles of your local supermarket. Together we can create new, dazzling and super-easy meals...IN NO TIME FLAT.

THE SHOPPING CART CHEF'S
15 COMMANDMENTS IN THE KITCHEN

MY **APOLOGIES** TO MOSES; HE MAY HAVE DONE IT IN **10**,
BUT HE WASN'T ASSEMBLING DINNER.

1. Approach the kitchen with a sense of humor.

2. If they make it better than you do, buy it.

3. Always mix in a container bigger than you need.

4. Use your tongs when you turn things...a fork releases those precious juices.

5. Quality ingredients reap their own culinary reward...Buy the best; buy seasonally; buy organic.

6. Taste as you go along and before serving to adjust seasonings.

7. Cheese, fruit, veggies and pastries all taste better @ room temperature.

8. Use your microwave for instant warm ups, melting and defrosting; it has a bad rap for no reason.

9. Always garnish the plate, platter or bowl. Be creative, not conventional; fresh herbs, flowers, Chinese five spice.

10. Meats cooked on the stove, in the oven, or outdoor grill need to rest 2-3 minutes before serving. All ready made proteins need to be room temperature prior to re-heating.

11. Great taste does not always translate to high fat.

12. Sharp knives save fingers; buy the best you can, sharpen often.

13. Remember, there is always more than one way to create something great on the plate.

14. The most used appliance in my kitchen? The toaster/oven/broiler. 9x15x11...sits on the counter; big enough to crisp half a chicken; small enough for a piece of toast...

15. Sometimes less is more, sometimes more is **WONDERFUL**.

THE
SHOPPING
CART CHEF

10 min

6 min

6 min

PIZZA PARADE
BRIES WITH EASE
A TRIO OF TRUFFLES
CREAM CHEESE IN A HULA SKIRT TWICE
TH3EE COCKTAIL QUICKIES
SUPER SOUR CITRUS COOLER
THE BEST NUT MIX OUTSIDE THE FAMILY

NIBBLES AND BEFORES

PIZZA PARADE

Thaw one sheet of frozen puff pastry.
With a sharp knife, cut it into thirds, then cut each strip into 6 triangles. Bake **triangles** at 375 for 12 minutes or until golden. Can be made a day in advance if stored airtight.
To serve, warm the **triangles** in a 350-degree oven for 5 minutes.
Top with the following combinations:

GREEN ON GREEN
Basil pesto from the refrigerated section
Fresh **basil leaves**, chopped
Toasted **pine nuts** (optional)

DOUBLE ARTICHOKE
Lemon artichoke pesto
Goat cheese, **Stilton** or **Danish blue**
Garnish with **artichoke hearts**, fresh **thyme** or **tarragon**

RED & BLACK
Sun **dried** **tomato** **pesto**
Ready made **olive bruschetta** (optional)
Garnish **with sun dried** tomatoes, sliced
Parmesan, shaved

PIZZA BOTTOMS
Today there is **flatbread**, **pita**, fresh **pizza dough**, ready made **thin crust** and regular **pizza rounds** that are naked. Mix and match the above tops with some new bottoms.
In Paris we had a truffle pizza with melted fontina, caramelized onions, and Nicoise olives. Yummmmmmm....

WANT ANOTHER HOT QUICKIE?
For personal pizzas, split a **mini pita bread** to make 2 rounds. Crisp them in a 400-degree oven, about 1 minute. Top with your choice of **pesto** and a sprinkle of any ready-shredded **Italian cheese blend**. Broil for another 2 minutes.

ALL CHEESE
SHOULD BE SERVED
ROOM TEMPERATURE
SO
THE
FLAVORS
BLOOOM

BRIES WITH EASE

Remove a whole round or wedge of **double** or **triple cream Brie** from the fridge and scrape top rind off with a paring knife or a cheese plane.

Allow Brie to come to room temperature and top with any of the following combinations:

- **Mango chutney** and **toasted slivered almonds**
- **Crumbled blue cheese** and **chopped salted pecans**
- **Ready made basil pesto** and **toasted pine nuts**
- **Sun-dried tomato pesto** and fresh **basil**

Enjoy 'Bries With Ease' on **crostini, mini rye** or any **cracker** you like.

FOODNOTES:
Never warm a Brie. When it cools it becomes like rubber cement.

Use up yesterday's **baguette** and make your own **crostini** ('little toasts').
Slice the bread into 1/4-inch disks, or at an angle.
Toast and store in an air tight container.

A TRIO OF TRUFFLES

BLACK GOLD (6 minutes serves 10)
Slice horizontally:
> One cold **8 oz. wedge** or **one whole round** of **Brie**, **double** or **triple cream**

Mix together:
> 2 parts *Urbani* **Salsa Tartufata**
> 1 part **cream cheese**

Like a layer cake, spread the above truffle mixture evenly over the bottom half of the **Brie** and replace the top half. Serve at room temperature with a seeded **baguette** and watch everyone swoon.

SERVING MUSHROOM SOUP? (6 minutes serves 1)
Heat:
> 8 oz. bowl of ready made **mushroom soup**.

Add a swirl of:
> **Crème fraiche**
> 1 tbsp. **Salsa Tartufata**

Garnish with **Italian parsley** or some fresh **dill**.

TRUFFLE PASTA (6 minutes serves 3-4)
Cook according to package directions:
> 9 oz. package fresh ready made **fettuccini, linguine** or **angel hair pasta** from the refrigerated section.

Toss immediately with:
> 3 tbsp. **olive**, or **truffle oil**
> 6 tbsp. **Salsa Tartufata**
> 1/2 C. **Parmesan** or **truffle cheese**, shaved or shredded

FOODNOTE:
Now there are minced truffles, truffle cheese and truffle oil, which make cooking with these luxurious fungi more affordable. You can find *Urbani* truffle products in upscale supermarkets and specialty stores.

RETHINK THE ORDINARY
MAKE IT
EXTRAORDINARY

CREAM CHEESE
IN a HULA-SKIRT *TWICE*

SAVORY
Mix together:
    1 pkg. (8 oz.) regular **cream cheese**
    1/4 C. chopped salted **pecans**
Roll into a log and refrigerate for about 30 minutes.

When ready to serve, roll in ready made **pesto** to coat, then roll in chopped fresh **basil**.

HOT/SWEET
Mix together:
    8 oz. **cream cheese**.
    1/4 C. chopped glazed **walnuts**
Roll in a log and refrigerate.

When ready to serve roll in **Emerald Sauce** (pg. 126), then roll it in chopped fresh **cilantro** and/or **mint**.

Serve either log on a platter with plenty of **crostini**, **crackers** or **mini breads**.

16

TH3EE COCKTAIL QUICKIES

As a "rule of 👍" for pates and cheeses:
Use 1 tbsp. for each hors d'oeuvre.

PUCKERY PATE

Seeded crackers or *Rubschlager* **cocktail breads and mini chips**
Marcel and Henri **Pate (pork, chicken, liver** or **truffle)**
Mango chutney
Pistachios

ITALIAN HOTTiE

Crostini
Goat cheese or a **creamy blue (Costello** or **Gorgonzola)**
Peppered Italian salami
Basil leaves

FOXY LOXY

Cucumber slice
Mascarpone or **cream cheese**
Smoked salmon
Ground **pepper**
Squirt of **lemon**
Fresh **dill**

SUPER SOUR CITRUS COOLER

For the basic 'cooler' combine in a pitcher or punch bowl:

    12 oz. **frozen lemonade concentrate**
    16 oz. **pink grapefruit juice**
    16 oz. of any one or a combination of:
    Ginger ale
    Grape juice
    Pomegranate juice
    Margarita mix

This cooler is intensely **citrus-y**, 'puckery' and **loved by all**.
THE KEY IS NO WATER.

BRUNCH?
Substitute the **lemonade concentrate** with frozen **orange juice concentrate**. Add **champagne** for a unique twist on a mimosa.

PARTY?
Offer some **tequila, rum** or **vodka.**
Make each glass gorgeous by garnishing with: **Berries**, **fresh mint** and **orange slices.**

OR Place whole **mint leaves** and **assorted berries** in an ice cube tray. Add **water** and freeze. Drop a few cubes into each glass or float them in your pitcher or punch bowl.

WHAT'S IN YOUR BOWL?

BEST NUT MIX OUTSIDE THE FAMILY

In a big bowl, mix together:
Chili peanuts
Wasabi peas
Sesame sticks
Assorted rice crackers
Salted Cashews, pecans, **walnuts, hazelnuts**
J.M. Macy's Cheesesticks, broken
OR whatever you fancy...

Make sure the combo is **colorful**, **spicy** and **nutty**. I am not a fan of raisins and cranberries, or anything sweet here. This is a savory mix, not a trail mix.

Make as much as you feel like, and freeze what you don't use for the next soiree.

FOODNOTES:
Today we can find wasabi peas in Cedar Rapids and rice crackers in Cleveland. It is just a big bore to serve salted peanuts, pretzels or chips. **Get creative**.

FREEZE YOUR NUTS...
They stay fresh for months and defrost in 60 seconds. This goes for the mixes with crackers too. You can reach in and take just what you need for garnishing a salad, or filling a nibble bowl.

TEQUILA LIME SHRIMP
CHUNKY TOMATO BASIL SOUP
10 MINUTE SHELLFISH CHOWDER
MINTY FETA SHRIMP
CHILI CON TRES VERDES
HOT TOMATO TART
BEIJING MEETS BROOKLYN IN A BOWL
AMERICAN CARPACCIO

SOUPS AND STARTERS

TEQUILA LIME SHRIMP

In a large bowl mix:

    3/4 C. **jarred green salsa,** well-drained (you pick the heat)
    1 1/2 tbsp. **lime juice**
    3 tbsp. **olive oil**
    2 tbsp. ready-chopped **red** or **white onion**

When you are ready to serve, toss in:

    2 tbsp. chopped fresh **cilantro**
    1 tbsp. **Tequila** (optional)
    20-25 large or jumbo cooked de-veined **shrimp**

Place **shrimp** on paper towels and squeeze the water out before tossing with the salsa.

Serve in chilled martini or shot glasses rimmed with **sea salt** or even better, with ***Urban Accents* Margarita Lime Salt**.

QUICKER NO LIQUOR...

Drain and measure the **salsa**. Add the chopped **onions** and **cilantro**. Serve with the shrimp or as a super-duper-chip-dipper.

CHUNKY TOMATO BASIL SOUP

GAZPACHO'S QUICKER, SLICKER COUSIN

Place in a food processor or blender:
>	3-4 C. colorful heirloom **tomatoes,** chopped and drained
>	10 fresh leaves of **basil**
>	2-3 tbsp. ready-chopped **onion**
>	3 tbsp. **Balsamic Glaze** (pg. 124) or
>	***Stonewall Kitchen's* Balsamic Fig Dressing**
>	Dash of **cayenne pepper**

Process until chunky. Careful not to over-process.

Garnish with:
>	**Crème fraiche** or **sour cream**
>	Fresh **basil**
>	**Croutons**

FOODNOTE:
A gorgeous, low-cal soup that's big on flavor, little on time.

10 MiNUTE SHELLFISH CHOWDER

In a large pot with a lid and 2 tbsp. water, steam:
> 24 total **mussels** and/or **clams** (about 5 minutes, be sure to discard any that don't open)

Add:
> 1 pint **clam chowder** from the hot soup station or seafood counter
> 1 8 oz. jar of **oysters** with their **juice**
> 15 raw **shrimp**, 'tails off'
> 2 tbsp. **Vermouth** (optional)

Simmer 5 minutes, be sure shrimp have turned pink, serve immediately. Garnish with **dill** or **parsley**.

Make it a meal with **Caesar's Uncle** (pg. 46) and **Pulled Bread** (pg. 100) or ready made **garlic bread**.

MINTY FETA SHRIMP

Scatter on a serving platter:
    3 C. **mixed** greens
    1/2 C. roughly-chopped fresh **mint**
Drizzle the salad with:
    1/4 C. **Simple Citrus Salad Dressing** (pg. 122) or
    BRIANNAS' **Real French Vinaigrette**
Place on top:
    24-30 large cooked **shrimp** (remove tails for easier eating)
    1/2 C. crumbled low-salt **feta** or **goat cheese**
    Handful of toasted **walnuts**
Garnish with a grind of fresh **black pepper**.

An assembly from the **bottom up**

FOODNOTE:
Lemon, mint, feta are a natural threesome. Add the **shrimp** and you have low-cal high-taste **perfection.**

CHILi CON TRES VERDES

Purchase one quart of your favorite **chili** from a restaurant or the hot soup station.
Divide and heat chili among 4 soup bowls.
Sprinkle each with 2 tbsp. ready-shredded **Mexican cheese blend**.
Put the bowls under a hot broiler for a minute or two.
Make sure cheese is melted and bubbly.

Quickly make a hole in the melted cheese and fill with:
> 1 tbsp. fresh or jarred drained **green salsa**, pick your **heat**
> 1 tbsp. fresh ready made **guacamole**

Garnish with:
> Chopped **cilantro**
> Chopped **green onions**

Serve with **blue corn** or classic **tortilla chips**, or a **naked taco shell**.

HOT TOMATO TART

Bake a naked **pie crust** according to package instructions.

Fill with below mixture:
> 3 C. diced fresh vine-ripened **tomatoes**, drained
> 3/4 C. **basil pesto** from the refrigerated section

Spread over the tomato mixture:
> 1/3-1/2 C. **mayonnaise**
> 3/4 C. ready-shredded **Italian cheese blend**

Place the baking dish on a foil-lined cookie sheet.
Bake in a 400 oven until browned and bubbly, 3-6 minutes.

Garnish with fresh **arugula**.

FOODNOTE:
Wanna skip the mayo and ~~the~~ calories...just use the cheese. *SOME OF*

BEIJING MEETS BROOKLYN *IN A BOWL*

Heat 2 quarts **Won Ton Soup** from your favorite local Chinese restaurant.

Add 3-4 C. **de-boned ready-roasted chicken** plus any **juices.**
Five minutes before serving throw in 20 medium-large cleaned, raw **shrimp**, tails-off. Cook until pink.

Need more liquid? Add 1 C. low-sodium **chicken broth**.
Garnish with **cilantro** or **Italian parsley**.

WANT MORE BROOKLYN?
Add 1 1/2 pints **matzo ball soup** from your favorite deli, or a 24 oz. jar.

* A quorum of ten men or women.

AMERICAN CARPACCIO*

APPETIZER
On each of 4 plates arrange:
> 3 or 4 slices rare **roast beef** from the deli section

Drizzle with:
> **Olive oil** and
> A grind of fresh **black pepper**

Top each plate with:
> A handful of torn **arugula** or **mixed baby lettuces**

Dress with:
> Simple Citrus Salad Dressing (pg. 122) or
> A drizzle of ***BRIANNAS'* Classic French Vinaigrette**

Garnish generously with:
> Shaved **Parmesan**,
> **Manchego** or **Asiago**

A TOPLESS TREAT
Toast 4-6 slices of **baguette, ciabatta** or **olive bread**.
Brush each slice with:
> **Olive oil**
> **Dijon mustard** or Simple Citrus Salad Dressing

Top with:
> A small handful of chopped **arugula**
> 3 or 4 slices of rare **roast beef**

Garnish with:
> 4 or 5 thin shavings of **Parmesan, Manchego** or **Asiago**
> Freshly ground **black pepper**

*Carpaccio** is a marvelous Italian appetizer made with paper-thin slices of raw beef.

SALADS

A PERFECT PEAR iN PaRIS

Cut two large **Belgian endive** lengthwise. Cut and discard bottoms and slice each half into thin strips. Scatter the slices on four plates.
Dress each plate with:
> **Simple Citrus Salad Dressing** (pg. 122) or your favorite ready made dressing

Cut 2 ripe **pears** in half, lengthwise. Remove the cores but leave skin on. Slice each half to create a fan. Top each salad with a **pear fan**.

Finish each plate with:
> 1 tbsp. crumbled **blue cheese**
> 1 tbsp. coarsely chopped **walnuts**

FOODNOTE:
I had forgotten about this sublime 5-ingredient classic until my husband and I recently enjoyed it at '**La Brasserie de l'Isle St. Louis**' in Paris. Leave it to the French; masters of the tongue and the table.

44

THE WORLD IS DIVIDED IN 2; THOSE WHO DELIGHT IN
CRISP SKIN, DARK MEAT & ANCHOVIES...
AND EVERYBODY ELSE.

CAESAR'S UNCLE

In the bottom of a salad bowl pour:
> 2-3 tbsp. **Julee's Caesar Salad Splash** from *The Silver Palate* thinned with a little **olive oil**.

Mix and match the following to make 4 C. total greens:
> **Frisee**
> **Arugala**
> **Belgian endive**
> **Baby greens**

Add:
> A handful of crushed **Caesar's Crisps** from *Just off Melrose*
> 1/2 tin drained and halved **anchovies** (silver skinned is best)
> 1 **soft boiled egg** (optional)

Toss and garnish with shaved **Parmesan** to serve.

WANT TO MAKE YOUR SALAD A MAIN DISH?
Add a generous 3/4 C. sliced or coarsely chopped **chicken** from a **ready-roasted bird**.

CASUALTHOUGHTS ON A SALAD TOSS

RULE OF 👍:

All mixtures below should add up to 4 cups if you want to serve 4 as a side salad. Pour 3-4 tbsp. dressing into the bottom of the bowl, add your greens then toss. Be creative; No specific proportions; Any combo you like best...including two or three, or four of your favorites from each.

HOT GREEK

In a bowl combine 4 tbsp. any **vinaigrette** with 1 tbsp. plain **yogurt**. Add and toss with:

>	**Broccoli slaw**, thin sliced **English cucumber**, **Belgian endive**, mixed **sprouts**, **fennel** (remove the hard core and slice), ready chopped **onions**, **dill** or **mint**, crumbled **feta**, **olive bruschetta** or **olive pesto**

GRASS AND SNOW

In a bowl combine crumbled **blue cheese**, **blue cheese dressing** (no sugar), and seasoned **croutons**. Add 4 C. of any of the following (chopped or torn) and toss:

>	**watercress**, **frisee**, **Bibb lettuce**, **snap peas**, **dill**, **Belgian endive**, **mixed sprouts**, sliced **green onions**, **hearts of palm**, or **water chestnuts**

ROMAINE HOLIDAY

In a bowl combine 1-2 tbsp. ready made refrigerated **basil pesto** with 2 tbsp. **Simple Citrus Salad Dressing** (pg. 122), or your favorite **caesar**. Add:

>	**Romaine hearts** and **basil** torn,
>	sliced **artichoke hearts** (seared if you want) and **arugula**

Garnish with:

>	chopped **prosciutto** or pan crisped **pancetta** and toasted **pine nuts**.

CHOP AND ROLL

Combine in a bowl and refrigerate for 10 minutes or up to 24 hours:
  1/4 C. **Citrus Soy Splash** (pg. 122)
  1 C. ready-chopped raw **vegetables**
  1 1/2 C. any **mixed grains salads** without fruit...how about:
  Brown rice, **couscous**, **quinoa**, **orzo** or **tabouli**

When ready to serve, pack mixture into 1/2 C. individual ramekins.
Turn ramekin upside down onto each serving plate. Tap the bottom until
it comes loose. No ramekins? Use a coffee cup and fill only half full.

Garnish with:
  Sprouts
  Italian parsley or
  Crushed salted **pecans**
Serve with:
  Toasted *Labrea Bakery* **whole grain** or **olive bread** and
  Chunks of *Laura Chenel* **chevre**

FAJITA CHOP

In a bowl combine:

   3 tbsp. **Simple Citrus Salad Dressing** (pg. 122)
   1/2 C. drained **green salsa**, pick your heat

Add and toss:

   One 14 oz. roughly chopped package **fajita mix** (ready-sliced **red onions**, tri-colored **bell peppers** and **cilantro**) from the produce department
   2 C. ready-cooked torn **chicken**
   2-3 handfuls mixed **baby lettuces** or **arugula**

WANT MORE KICK?

Add your favorite **hot sauce**, or a couple of dashes of **cayenne pepper**.

FOODNOTE:
A loose and lanky luncheon or poolside main dish. Serve this salad as a colorful side with a bowl of **Chili Con Tres Verdes** (pg. 34).

HEIRLOOM TOMATO
CELEBRATiON

Slice and layer on four plates from the bottom up:
   3-4 large colorful **heirloom tomatoes**
   2 thin slices or 1 tbsp. ready diced **sweet onion** per plate
   10 fresh **basil leaves**, thinly sliced

Drizzle the plates with:
   4-5 tbsp. **Balsamic Glaze** (pg. 124) or
   Off the shelf **balsamic vinaigrette**

Garnish each plate with one or two of the following:
   1 tsp. **Bella Cucina** **Olive Pesto** or
   Nicoise olives pitted and chopped
   1 **anchovy**
   Crumbled **goat cheese**
   Crushed unsalted **pecans** (**optional**)

FOODNOTE:
The evolution of today's great tasting and glorious tomatoes makes this ordinary salad sing...the availability of an array of olives, cheeses and fresh herbs is an example of our super duper markets of today.

54

LOBSTER &
LEMONAISE

BUSINESS CLASS

For a seafood salad with sass use any combination of:

2-3 C. fresh cooked **lobster**, **crab meat** and **shrimp**,

1-2 C. **mixed baby greens**, with

1 tbsp. fresh **dill**, and or **tarragon**; save some for garnish.

Dress lightly, tossing from the bottom of the bowl up with:

2 tbsp. *Ojai Cook* **Lemonaise*** or **Lemonaise with Garlic and Herbs**, both available at Whole Foods.

2 tbsp. our **Simple Citrus Salad Dressing**, (pg. 122) or your favorite off the shelf **vinaigrette**.

Garnish with a piece of **lobster**, **crab** or whole **shrimp**, and **dill**. Serve with a wedge of **lemon** and fresh ground **black pepper**, and toasted **sourdough**.

FIRST CLASS

Same proportions, but use only **lobster**.

PRIVATE JET

Give each serving a super duper upgrade with a dollop of **salmon roe** or **black caviar**.

***NO LEMONAISE**?

Mix together:

3 tbsp. mayonnaise

1 tsp. lemon juice

FRESH ORANGE SALSA
& TWO CLOSE COUSINS

Perfect partners with **chicken**, **duck**, **pork**, and **grains**.

FRESH ORANGE SALSA
Mix together:
- 1 C. diced and drained fresh **orange segments**
- 3 tbsp. ready-chopped **red onion**,
- 3 tbsp. dried **cranberries,** (optional)
- 2 tbsp. chopped fresh **cilantro**, or **basil** or half and half
- 1 tbsp. **olive oil**
- A good shake of **cayenne pepper**

TWO CLOSE COUSINS:

SUNNY WITH SPICE
Mix together:
- 3 tbsp. **Intense Orange Vinaigrette***
- 1 C. **Fresh Orange Salsa** (above) or
- 1 C. fresh ready made **mango salsa** with
- 2 C. ready-roasted **beet salad** from the prepared food section

EAST/WEST ORANGE SALAD
Toss 3-4 tbsp. **Intense Orange Vinaigrette** with any combination: (3 C. total)
- Thin sliced **bok choy**, **green onion**, **torn watercress**,
- **dikon**, any **mixed sprouts**, **Bibb lettuce**, sliced **water chestnuts**

Add:
- 1 C. **Fresh Orange Salsa** (above)
- A handful glazed **walnuts**

*__*Intense Orange Vinaigrette__
- 3 tbsp. **Simple Citrus Salad Dressing** (pg. 122)
- 1 tbsp. frozen **orange juice**

UPDATE ON HERBS

DRIED HERBS ARE DEAD

Fresh herbs are an instant face lift to everything. They heighten the flavor and garnish the plate. You can grow them or buy them anywhere, and there are at least 20 I haven't mentioned.

ITALIAN PARSLEY: Mild versatile flavor. More sophisticated cousin of regular parsley. Chop and use to spruce up anything from pasta to french fries. Great to garnish a plate or platter.

CILANTRO: Bold distinct flavor. Rarely cook. Marries well with onions and citrus. Mandatory in fresh salsa. Adds a distinct flavor to Indian, Asian and Latin foods.

BASIL: Peppery and robust. Great addition to many salads; sliced or as garnish...the base of classic ready made Mediterranean pesto.

ROSEMARY: Very fragrant and intense...use sparingly; adds great dimension to meats, chops, chicken and potatoes.

DILL: Mild licorice flavor. Graceful garnish on grilled or ready poached fish and chilled seafood...Mixes well with mayo...Nice surprise in green salads as well.

MINT: Fresh, clean, immensely versatile. Naturally pairs with sweet and savory dishes. Think ready roasted lamb with mint jelly and fresh mint; or mint with fresh fruit and mint chip ice cream.

WATERCRESS: Crunchy, with a crisp, mustard-like bite adds character to salads, sandwiches, cold soup...Great as a garnish.

FOODNOTES:
If I were getting married tomorrow this would be my wedding bouquet; I would throw in a few edible flowers for color.

Serving a special dinner with some herbs in the menu choices? They would be wonderful as a row of 'interesting greens' in simple glasses down the middle of the table.

SMOKED SALMON WITH CRUNCHY GREENS
TARTINE CHEZ MOI
THE ITALIAN STALLION
GRILLED CHEESE FOR GROWNUPS
CHICKEN WINNER SANDWICH
BILLY'S BOYHOOD BEST

SANDWICHES
BETWEEN **THE** SLICES **AND** TOPLESS TREATS

SMOKED SALMON
WITH CRUNCHY GREENS

TWICE

SMOKED SALMON SANDWICH
Assemble each open-facer from the bottom up:
> 1 slices of fresh **rye bread** (toasted or not)
> 1 tbsp. **creamy goat cheese** mixed with
> 1 tbsp. *Krinos* Taramosalata
> 1 tsp. chopped **dill**

Top with:
> 2-3 slices **smoked salmon** per sandwich
> A good grind of **pepper** & a squirt of lemon

Garnish with **greens** as much or little as you want:
Chives, **cucumber slices**, ready chopped **onion**, **watercress** and **dill**.

AN ELEGANT APPETIZER
On each plate assemble from the bottom up:
> 2-3 slices **smoked salmon**
> 2-3 tbsp. **tarama cream*** drizzled
> A generous grind of **pepper**

Dress plate with **greens** from Smoked Salmon Sandwich. (above)
Serve with a warm crusty **baguette**.

*Tarama cream:
> 1/2 C. **sour cream**
> 1/2 C. *Krinos* **Taramosalata** a greek caviar found in the refrigerated section of many speciality stores
> 2 tbsp. chopped **dill**,
> 1 tbsp. **lemon juice**

FOODNOTE:
Smoked salmon can be found everywhere, but the best we ever tasted is from *Michel Cordon Bleu*. It's easily purchased on-line, and at speciality food stores.

TARTINE CHEZ MOi

Toast 4 slices of **mixed grain**, **olive**, **sourdough** or **brown bread**
Top with:
>	**Goat cheese**
>	Ready-roasted **peppers** from the prepared food section
No roasted peppers?
Sear in a hot pan:
>	1 package **fajita mix** from the produce section
>	2-3 tbsp. **Citrus Soy Splash** (pg. 122)

WANNA BE 'TRES FRANCAIS?'
Top each tartine with a fried **egg** and an **anchovy**

FOODNOTE:
Tartine' is an open-faced sandwich. This simple glorious example was introduced to us in March 2009 in Paris. There are zillions of combos that qualify: fromage, legumes cuits, jambon, paté...au bon pain.

THE ITALIAN STALLION

For this open-facer purchase from the fresh bakery department:
> Two **ciabatta**
> **Multi grain** or
> *Labrea Bakery* **seeded** or **olive rolls**

Slice horizontally and brush with:
> **Olive oil**
> **Coarse mustard**
> **Basil pesto** from the refrigerated section

Sprinkle generously with:
> **3 cheese Italian blend** or **shaved Parmesan**

Broil for 2-3 minutes until cheese melts before topping with:
> 4-6 slices **Italian dry** or **peppered salami**, or **sopressetta**
> 2 slices **prosciutto**
> A few shaves of **Parmesan**

For color and crunch tuck in some **arugula** or **mixed lettuces**.
Finish with a good grind of fresh black **pepper**.
Assemble and serve quickly while the cheese is hot.

Yummy with our **Romaine Holiday Salad**. (pg. 48)

ARE YOU A FOOD LEMMING?

STOP RUNNING IN THE SAME OLD CULINARY DIRECTION.

GRILLED CHEESE FOR GROWNUPS

In any order you want, layer the below sandwiches, beginning and ending with the **chutney**, **mustard** or **tapenade**. Grill in a very hot pan with a bit of **butter** or **oil**, 2-3 minutes each side.

- **Mango chutney**, chopped **green onions**, sliced **chicken** and **gruyere** on **whole grain bread**.

- *Stonewall Kitchen's* **Farmhouse Chutney**, aged **cheddar**, toasted **pecans**, on grilled **sourdough**.

- *Silver Palate's* **Sweet and Rough Mustard**, thin sliced **smoked ham**, **jarlesberg** on **rye**.

- *Bella Cucina's* **Olivada Olive Pesto**, with **prosciutto** and **Fontina** on **olive**, or **three seed bread**.

- *Stonewall Kitchen's* **Fig Raisin Chutney**, *Cypress Grove's* **Humboldt Fog**, **arugula** on **raisin nut toast**.

Cut them in half and serve for a sophisticated lunch with one of our salads, **OR** slice the sandwiches into bite size pieces and serve as hors d'oeuvres.

FOODNOTE:
These sandwiches reflect the vast selections available, and easily assembled from today's supermarkets. Have fun. Mix and match some exotic breads and fillings.

WE LIKE TOPLESS SANDWICHES... YOU CAN SEE WHAT YOU'RE EATING & EXIT THAT EXTRA SLICE OF BREAD.

CHICKEN WINNER
SANDWICH

Start with four slices **country white** or **sourdough toast.**
Spread with a mixture of:
>   2 tbsp. **lemon juice**
>   1/2 C **mayonnaise**
>   1/2 C chopped **cilantro**
>   2 tbsp. **artichoke** pesto or **guacamole.**

Crown with 3 or 4 slices **chicken** per sandwich from ready cooked chicken breasts.

Garnish with:
>   Chopped salted **pecans** (optional) and
>   **Cilantro sprigs**

Messy, use a really sharp knife to cut.

A sandwich from the bottom up

(left to right) **Billy K.**, **Billy Vogel**, **Jo-Ann L.**, **Bobby M.**, **Steve S.**

MY husband grew up in New York City and he was lucky enough to go to Camp 'WelMet' every summer with a bunch of good buddies. When Billy went to Liberty NY to see the doctor, dentist or whatever, his big treat was to get a sacred sandwich from a little take out place. They always had a line around the block, but it was worth the wait...hot Chinese roast pork on a toasted garlic roll. He swoons everytime I mention those Asian gems.

BILLY'S BOYHOOD
BEST

Slice and toast four soft **rolls** and spread each half with:
>   **Garlic butter** (or purchase ready made **garlic bread**)

Then brush toast with:
>   Jarred **sweet and sour sauce** or
>   The original *Saucy Susan* **peach apricot sauce**

Distribute on the garlic toast:
>   1 lb. ready made **Chinese roast pork**, sliced

Before closing, add some:
>   Fresh **cilantro** and
>   Chopped **green onions**

FOODNOTE:
For a quickie supper serve with **Nutty Ginger Slaw** (pg. 84) or **East/West Orange Salad** (pg. 58).

CITRUS MUSTARD CHICKEN
CRISPY CHICK WITH TARRAGON & SAGE
NAKED RIBS WITH 3 DRESSES
HOT BIRD ON A BED OF SUPER SLAW
ONE COLD FISH 2WO SAUCES
PASTA PERFECT 3 TIMES
COOKIE'S QUICK COQ AU VIN
ROAST PORK WITH DRIED FRUIT
THE PERFECT STEAK ON A PLATE
SEARED TUNA WITH WASABI SPLASH

ROAST SMASHED POTATOES
PULLED BREAD
INFINITE ASPARAGUS OR GREATER GREEN BEANS

MEATS, MAINS, AND SIDES

CITRUS MUSTARD CHICKEN

Purchase a cooked **rotisserie chicken**.
Leave it whole or cut it into 4 or 6 pieces.

Mix together:
> 1/2 C. **coarse** mustard
> 1/2 C. orange **marmalade**

Brush the mixture all over the **chicken**.
Broil with the skin-side up until crisp and brown for about 3-5 minutes.
Garnish with:
> **Lime wedges** and
> Fresh **rosemary**.

To serve four, purchase 2–2 1/2 C. **wild rice salad** from the salad bar
or prepared foods section.
As another option, any **mixed grain salad** with **fruit** will do
(**cranberries**, **raisins**, **oranges**…etc.)

OR

Serve with **East/West Orange Salad** or **Sunny with Spice**. (pg. 58)

SOMETIMES iT'S ~~OK~~ FUN TO LICK YOUR FINGERS

CRISPY CHICK
WITH TARRAGON AND SAGE

Start with 1 **ready-roasted chicken** in 8-10 pieces.
Remove all bones but leave the skin on as best you can.
Messy and imperfect is delicious. Fewer calories; remove the skin.

Place chicken (skin side down) in a pan and sear for 3-5 minutes until
brown and crisp, with:
> 2-3 tbsp. **Citrus Soy Splash** (pg. 122)
> 2 tbsp. fresh chopped **sage leaves** (optional)
> 2 tbsp. **tarragon**

Add the fresh herbs in the last 2 minutes.
Serve chicken, crispy side up, with pan juices and herbs on a platter with:
> 2-3 C. **couscous**, **noodles**, **rice**, **ready-grilled veggies** from the
> prepared food department or the salad bar (nothing sweet).

Garnish with:
> 2-3 tbsp. additional **Citrus Soy Splash** if necessary
> 2-3 tbsp. fresh **tarragon leaves** chopped

NAKED RiBS WITH 3 DRESSES

Purchase 16 oz. ready-cooked **beef** or **pork ribs,** without sauce (if possible), from your favorite neighborhood rib joint or supermarket. If sauced, wipe off as much as you can.

Wrap in foil and warm in the oven or grill over low-burning coals for 5 minutes. Turn over and heat 5 minutes more.

Just before serving, dress with one of the following sauces or serve all three on the side and let your guests choose:

BLACK LACQUER BBQ SAUCE (pg. 124)

FIRECRACKER BBQ SAUCE (pg. 124)

CITRUS SOY SPLASH (pg. 122)

FOODNOTES:
Serve with a pile of paper napkins and our **Nutty Ginger Slaw** (pg. 84), **Sunny with Spice** (pg. 58) or **Grass and Snow**. (pg. 48)

HOT BiRD
ON A BED OF SUPER SLAW

Purchase 1 quartered ready-roasted **Chinese duck**.
Warm duck skin-side up in a 400 degree oven until crispy and brown, about 6 minutes. Make sure duck is room temp before re-heating.

NUTTY GINGER SLAW
Mix together:
> 1/2 C. ***BRIANNAS' Mandarin Ginger Dressing*** with:
> 1 12 oz. bag of undressed **broccoli slaw**
> 3-4 tbsp. ready-chopped **onion**
> 1/4 C. chopped fresh **cilantro**
> 1/2 C. salted chopped **peanuts** or **almonds**.

Divide the salad on four plates and top each plate with a piece of crispy **duck** and a sprig of **cilantro**.

WANT MORE FUN?
Add some chopped **candied ginger**.

ONE COLD FiSH 2WO SAUCES

Purchase 1 lb. ready-poached **salmon** from the Fresh Seafood Department. Cut into 4 pieces and divide among 4 plates. Drizzle with either of the following sauces:

CITRUS & SASS
Combine:
> 1/2 C. *Ojai Cook* **Lemonaise** or **Lemonaise with Garlic and Herbs** (available at Whole Foods) thinned with 1 tbsp. **olive oil**

No Lemonaise? Mix together:
> 1/2 C. **mayonnaise**
> 1 tbsp. **lemon** or lime **juice**
> 1 tsp. **mustard**

Drizzle dressing on each portion of salmon and garnish with:
> **Red** and **black pepper**,
> Chopped fresh **dill** &
> **Red caviar** (optional)

Serve with a lemon wedge on a bed of fresh chopped **watercress** or mixed **baby greens**.

GREEN WITH ENVY
Drizzle the poached **salmon** with **Emerald Sauce** (pg. 126) instead of lemon/mayo sauce.

Serve with **East West Orange Salad** (pg. 58) minus the **Fresh Orange Salsa**. Garnish fish and salad with extra chopped **mint** and **cilantro**.

PASTA PERFECT
3 TiMES

ARTICHOKE LEMON PASTA

Cook according to package directions:
>9 oz. fresh ready made **angel hair**, **linguine** or
>**fettucini pasta** from the refrigerated section.

Drain and toss while still very hot with:
>An 8 oz. container prepared **artichoke lemon pesto.**

Sprinkle with some **Parmesan** and/or **Gorgonzola**.
Garnish with **chives** and **basil**.

NEW TOMATO PASTA

Follow same directions for making **Artichoke Lemon Pasta**
except drain and toss with:
>One 8 oz. container of prepared **sun dried tomato pesto.**

OR
>4 oz. **tomato pesto**
>4 oz. **mixed olive and red pepper bruschetta** and
>1 tbsp. **olive oil** (if too thick)

For an unusual garnish, sear some fresh **baby tomatoes** in a very hot
pan with some **olive oil**.

GREEN, EASY & CHEESY

Cook according to package directions:
>9 oz. any ready made fresh cheese **tortellini** from the
>refrigerated section.

Toss with:
>6 tbsp. **basil pesto** from the refrigerated section
>1/2 C. cooked chopped **baby broccoli** and
>Chopped fresh **basil**

Garnish with ready-shredded **Italian cheese blend** or fresh grated
Parmesan.

COOoKIE'S QUICK COQ AU ViN

This dish is so delicious and it only takes 20 minutes rather than 2 hours.

Microwave for 3-4 minutes:
> 2-3 C. ready chopped packaged fresh **veggies**. Such as:
> **Mushrooms**, **broccoli**, **carrots**, **onions**, **leeks**.

In an oven proof serving dish, put the veggies with:
> 1 tbsp. **rosemary**, **tarragon**, or **thyme** (or all three), chopped
> 1/2 ready-cooked **chicken** cut into 6 or 8 pieces and de boned
> 3/4 C. **white wine**,
> 1/2 C. **Citrus Soy Splash**. Mix it all up.

Everything is already cooked so just heat in a 350 degree oven for 15 minutes. Before you serve add more **wine**, **herbs**, **chicken**, **veggies**; whatever it needs to be fabulous. Pop back in the oven to serve piping hot. Garnish with a sprig of **rosemary**. Serve with a warm crusty **sour-dough baguette** to soak up the savory juices.

CHICKEN POT PIE PUFF

Cut out a piece of defrosted **puff pastry**. Roll out to be 2 inches bigger than the **Coq Au Vin dish**. Cook naked until puffed and brown on a cookie sheet according to package directions. Add ½ C. hot **cream** to the Coq. Put the puff on top. Pop in the oven another 5 minutes and serve.

HOW ABOUT A BUTTERMILK BISCUIT HAT?

Just roll out 3-4 **buttermilk biscuits** into one piece to fit the chicken dish. Cook separately according to package directions and serve the hat on the hot chick.

ROAST PORK WITH DRIED FRUIT
& BALSAMIC GLAZE

Roughly chop and place in a microwaveable bowl:
>2 C. **Mariani** **Dried Fruits** (**pears, apricots, plums, nectarines, cranberries**)

Add:
>3/4-1 C. **Balsamic Glaze** (pg. 124)

Microwave for 2-3 minutes and pour over:
>1 lb. ready-cooked slow roasted **pork** (sometimes called '**carnitas**') from the hot prepared foods section.

Meat should be warm and juicy when serving.

Serve with any ready made sweet and savory side. Try **wild rice salad, couscous** with **cranberries**, roasted **sweet potatoes** or **golden and red beet salad**…etc.

Garnish with **mint**.

THE PERFECT
STEAK ON A PLATE

2 lb. boneless **rib eye** seasoned on both sides with salt and pepper (3-1 ratio) or ***Urban accents* Chicago Steak and Chop rub**, or a hearty brush of **Citrus Soy Splash**. (pg. 122)
Meat should be room temperature.

Sear both sides for 1 1/2 minutes in a very hot pan (cast iron is the best) or over mature coals. Turn with tongs. Remove from heat and let rest 6-7 minutes. Back on the grill, or in the pan; 3-4 minutes each side for medium rare...depending on the thickness of the steak. The firmer to the touch the more it is done. Let it rest 4-5 minutes.

Drizzle and garnish with:
> **Pan juices** and a pat of **butter**
> An additional brush of **Citrus Soy Splash**, (pg. 122) warmed
> Chopped **rosemary**

Great with **Roast Smashed Potatoes** (pg. 98), **Greater Green beans** (pg. 102), **Caesars Uncle** (pg. 46), and **grilled onions**.

FOODNOTES:
BUY THE BEST...we like rib eye..but as long as it is prime and very well marbled it should be great: bright red meat, not much juice: beef should be firm to the touch.

WHATEVER HAPPENED TO GOOD TABLE MANNERS?

DID THEY DISAPPEAR WHEN TV DINNERS CAME IN?

SEARED TUNA WITH WASABI SPLASH

Place in a large mixing bowl:
>4 to 5 tbsp. **Simple Citrus Salad Dressing** (pg. 122)

With 4 C. any combination of:
>**Mixed greens**
>**Arugula**
>Sliced **fennel**
>**Watercress**
>1 tbsp. chopped **green onions**

Divide salad evenly among 4 dinner plates and top each with:
>1/4 lb. fresh seared **tuna*** from the prepared foods section

Drizzle with a mixture of:
>1/2 C. **Citrus Soy Splash** (pg. 122)
>2 tsp. **wasabi**

Garnish with fresh **dill** or **cilantro**.

*NO READY-SEARED TUNA?

Sear your own in a very hot non-stick pan sprayed with oil, 2 1/2 minutes on each side.

OVERCOOK YOUR TUNA?

Make a classic tuna salad and you'll never eat canned again.

ROAST SMASHED POTATOES
WITH ROSEMARY, GRUYERE OR MANCHEGO

In a bowl put 1 lb. ready roasted **potatoes** from the prepared foods section. Smash the potatoes with a potato masher or fork and toss with:

    1 tbsp. chopped fresh **rosemary**

    1 C. grated **gruyere** or **manchego** (1/2 C. to toss and 1/2 C. to melt)

Mash the mixture in a hot pan with 2 tbsp. **butter**. Cook until crisp and brown. Turn like a pancake; scatter additional cheese on top. Cover pan and cook a few minutes until underside gets brown and top cheese is melted.

Cut into 4 equal pieces and serve with **steak**, crispy **chicken**, or seared **tuna**. A little rich but quite yummmmmy.

HAVE FUN
WITH
YOUR FOOOOD

PULLED BREAD
WITH CONFETTI BUTTER & DYNAMITE DIPPING OIL

Purchase a good crusty loaf such as **olive**, **sourdough**, **whole grain** or **French**. Tear into fist-sized pieces, each with a bit of crust intact. Dip the ragged inside edge into either the **Confetti Butter** or **Dynamite Dipping Oil** and lay facing up on a cookie sheet. Broil until light brown and serve immediately.

CONFETTI BUTTER
Melt 1 stick **salted butter** and add:
> 1-2 tbsp. fresh **lemon juice**
> 1 tbsp. **stone ground mustard**
> 2 tbsp. fresh minced **herbs,** use one, two or three of these:
> **Thyme**, **rosemary**, **oregano**, **tarragon**, **parsley**

DYNAMITE DIPPING OIL
> 1 C. good **olive oil**
> 1/2 tsp. jarred minced **garlic**
> 1-2 tsp. minced **herbs**; choose from above. (optional)
> 3-4 tbsp. any hard cheese, finely shredded;
> How about **Manchego** or aged **white cheddar**?

FOODNOTES:
The dipping oil and confetti butter are also great with a fresh crusty bread at any meal; no broiling necessary.

When serving put dipping oil or melted confetti butter on the table. Just shake the jar and pour into a ramekin for dipping.

Both bread partners keep very well for two weeks in the fridge. Either is an amazingly versatile flavor booster. They can be tossed with anything savory; from cooked greens to fresh pasta.

INFINITE ASPARAGUS OR GREATER GREEN BEANS

Snip, snap or cut ends off:
> 1/2 lb. **asparagus** or
> Fresh **green beans**

Steam for 6 minutes or microwave for 2 minutes.
Briefly toss the asparagus or green beans in a hot pan with
> 1-2 tbsp **Confetti Butter** (pg. 100)

When ready to serve garnish with:
> Toasted **pine nuts** and
> Fresh ground **pepper**

MORE QUICKIES:

- Toss with ready made **sun dried tomato** or **basil pesto** thinned with a little **olive oil**.

- Sprinkle with **Fontina** and melt.

- Serve cold; drizzle with our **Simple Citrus Salad Dressing** (pg. 122) or one of your bottled favorites. Garnish with 2 tbsp. chopped **chives**, **tarragon** or **dill** and a handful of chopped salted **pecans**.

- How about draping a couple slices of **prosciutto** over each plate of room temperature dressed **skinny greens** for a swell starter.

Finish any of the above with a drizzle of dressing and a coarse grind of **pepper** and 6 crushed *Just off Melrose* Caesar Crisps.

CALIFORNIA CITRUS CAKE
CHOCOLATE AND *CIAO BELLA*
DEEP, DARK, BUMPY BARK
ENDLESS TOPTIONS CHEESECAKE
GINGER CARAMEL COFFEE CRUNCH
INSTANT TARTLETS
AMERICAN PIE (SUMMER AND WINTER)

SWEET TREATS TO EAT

WHY BOTHER BAKING?

CALIFORNIA CITRUS CAKE

Defrost one naked, **all-butter pound cake** and place in a large pan with sides. Poke deep holes all over the top with a skewer.

Microwave the following for 15-20 seconds:
>1/2 C. **brown sugar**
>5 tbsp. lemon or lime **juice**

Drizzle the **syrup** mixture all over top, sides and bottom of the cake. Then roll the sticky cake in **brown sugar** (coverage will be spotty).

Slice and serve on a platter with:
>**Fruit** or **berries**
>**Whipped cream**

Garnish with a sprig of **mint**.

WANT SOME EXTRA CRUNCH?
Sprinkle the top with 1/2 C. of ready packaged, glazed **walnuts** or **pecans**, coarsely chopped.

CHOCOLATE &
CiaO BELLA
WITH COCOA & CAYENNE

Purchase:
    Individual **flourless chocolate cakes**
    A whole **flourless chocolate cake** (frozen or fresh) or
    A tray of uncut brownies.

If necessary cut out individual chocolate cakes with a cookie or biscuit cutter. Cake should be cold, cutter should be warmed under hot water and dried.

Warm cakes before serving so the center is creamy and dreamy.

Serve on individual plates with a scoop of *Ciao Bella* **sorbet**.
Try **mango**, **passion fruit** or **blood orange**.

Sprinkle with **cocoa** and a pinch of **cayenne** for some chocolate heat.

Garnish with a **flower** or fresh **mint**.

DEEP DARK BUMPY BARK

Melt according to package instructions:
    Two 11.5 oz. bags of 60% **cocoa bittersweet** premium
    chocolate baking chips
Stir until smooth and completely melted.

Add 10-12 oz. or 1 1/2 C. chopped **dried fruits**, choose 2 or 3;
or one fruit and one nut:
    Golden raisins,
    Dried cranberries,
    Diced **candied ginger** (a must),
    Candied orange peel
    3-4 shakes **cayenne pepper** and/or
    A generous shake of **Chinese five spice**
    Roughly chopped unsalted **hazelnuts** or **pecans**

Pour the mixture onto a 6 x 8 mini-baking sheet lined with plastic
wrap. Cool at room temperature until hard. Break into chunks or cut
into squares. Store at room temperature in a cool, dry place.

FOODNOTES:
Be sure there is not a drop of moisture anywhere in this assembly or the
chocolate won't set.

We have discovered a one stop baking needs shop, **N.Y. Cake**,
visit on-line (NYCake.com) or at their stores in LA and NYC.
Great accessories for molding and holding your easy chocolate assemblies.

ENDLESS TOPTIONS
CHEESECAKE

Defrost a frozen **cheesecake** according to package directions, leave whole or cut into slices. Mix or match the following toptions:

- Dash of **cinnamon** or a pinch of **Chinese Five Spice**

- Chopped glazed **walnuts** or **pecans**

- Chopped fresh mango

- Shredded **coconut**

- **Sultry Citrus Sauce** (pg. 128)

- **Pomegranate seeds** and dried **cranberries** soaked in **red wine** or **Crème de Cassis**, then drained.

- Fresh **berries** of your choice

Garnish whole cake or individual pieces with **mint sprig**.

FANCY SCHMANCY
Make instant mini cakes with a round biscuit or cookie cutter. Cheesecake needs to be very cold, but not frozen. Cutter needs to be warm an dry (heat under hot water and dry). You can always reform or smooth the sides with a knife if your cake is messy.

3MIN
SERVES
1

GINGER CARAMEL
COFFEE CRUNCH

In a parfait glass or goblet assemble from the bottom up:
- 1 crushed **ginger cookie**
- 1 tbsp. **caramel sauce**
- 1 tbsp. **English toffee pieces**
- 1 tsp. minced fresh **mint** (optional)
- 2 modest scoops **coffee** or **caramel ice cream**

Top with more:
- **Caramel sauce**
- **English toffee pieces**
- **Gingerbread cookie**

Garnish with a sprig of fresh **mint**.

Don't weigh yourself 'til the day after tomorrow.

INSTANT TARTLETS

Purchase your favorite all-butter **shortbread cookies**, *Walker's* **Round Shortbread** or **Stem Ginger Biscuits** make perfect bottoms.

Decorate each round with fresh seasonal **fruits** and **berries**.

Drizzle each tartlet with **Sultry Citrus Sauce**. (pg. 128)

OR any all natural thick **fruit spread** or **jam** thinned with a bit of **lemon** or **lime juice**...approx. 1/2 C. jam, 1/2-1 tsp. juice.

FOODNOTE:
Dinner is finished, everything was divine but no one wants a big, gooey dessert. They'll only eat it and feel guilty...or not eat it and hurt your feelings. **Instant Tartlets** are the perfect solution.

116

AMERICAN PiE

Bake your favorite **pie crust** naked until light brown, then cool until room temperature. May be baked ahead. Refrigerate over night and then bring to room temperature.

SUMMER FRUIT PiE
Cut or slice 4 C. including whatever is available and ripe:
>   **berries**, sliced **nectarines**,
>   **peaches**, **plums**,
>   **mango**, **figs**, etc.

Toss with:
>   1/2-2/3 C. **Sultry Citrus Sauce** (pg. 128)

Fill the pie just before serving to keep crust crisp. If needed, brush on a bit more glaze. Garnish with **mint**.

FOODNOTE:
This pie serves like a cobbler, so it is messy and yummy.
Not so fattening unless you insist on ice cream too.

WINTER FRUIT TART
Mix:
>   2 C. drained, canned, or jarred **cherries**,
>   2 C. dried **mixed fruits** (we love *Mariani* brand) **cranberries**,
>   chopped **apricots**, **pears**, **nectarines**, **figs**, **apples**.

Soak the mixture overnight in:
>   2 C. **Port** and/or **cranberry juice** to cover

When everything is soft, drain and bind fruits with:
>   1/2 C. of chunky **blueberry**, **plum**, or **cherry jam**
>   2 tbsp. **lemon juice** and
>   1 tbsp. **port** or **fruit liquor**. (optional)

Fill the baked crust and brush with additional **fruit glaze**, if necessary.
Serve within two hours so the crust doesn't sog or sag.

Garnish with ready-glazed, chopped **walnuts** before serving. (optional)

SIMPLE CITRUS SALAD DRESSING
CITRUS SOY SPLASH
BALSAMIC GLAZE
FIRECRACKER BBQ SAUCE
BLACK LACQUER BBQ SAUCE
TEQUILA LIME SALSA
EMERALD SAUCE
SULTRY CITRUS SAUCE
SUPER SOUR SUGAR SYRUP
NEW THOUGHTS ON A CHOCOLATE SAUCE

WET ONES
SAUCES AND SUCH

BOOKMARK
I'LL
SEND
YOU
HERE
OFTEN

CITRUS DRESSING & SOY SPLASH

SIMPLE CITRUS SALAD DRESSING

Mix, jar and refrigerate: (easy to double)
> 1/2 C. **olive** or **canola oil** or a mixture of both
> 1 1/2 tbsp. each **lemon juice**,
> 1 1/2 tbsp. **stone ground** or **whole grain mustard**
> **Salt** and **pepper** to taste

For color and flavor add one or two just before tossing:
> 1 tsp. each chopped **tarragon**, **dill**, **chives** & **Italian parsley**

For a creamier vinaigrette add 1 tbsp. **mayonnaise.**

How to get dressed...
Place the dressing in the bowl first, then the **greens**.
1 tbsp. **dressing** to 2 C. **salad greens** is a good place to start.
You can always add more dressing.
Toss from the bottom up.

CITRUS SOY SPLASH

THE universal savory sauce and flavor enhancer...

Mix, jar and refrigerate the above citrus dressing (minus the salt) with:
> 1 tbsp. **soy sauce**

Use as a marinade, brush on before cooking or before serving. Pumps up the flavor of everything savory from **fish** to **lamb** to cooked **veggies**.

GREENOTE:
Recycle your empty pickle and relish jars to mix, jar and refrigerate your sauces and dressings.

MAiNLY MEAT SAUCES

BALSAMIC GLAZE
Mix, jar and refrigerate:
>1/4 C. **maple syrup**
>1/4 C. **balsamic vinegar**
>3 tbsp. **Port**, **red wine**, **pomegranate** or **grape juice**
>2 tbsp. **olive oil**
>2 tbsp. **coarse mustard**.

FOODNOTES:
A hot, sweet sauce that won't fry your lips but may make you drool a bit. Originally created for **Roast Pork with Dried Fruits**. (pg. 92) Makes a spectacular salad drizzle, or dressing.

FIRECRACKER BBQ SAUCE
Mix, jar and refrigerate.
>2/3 C. **orange marmalade**
>2 tbsp. **white vinegar**
>1 tsp. jarred or fresh minced **garlic**.

FOODNOTES:
Different from the usual tomato-based barbeque sauce. Try for a uniquely yummy change of pace. Keeps 2 months in the fridge.

BLACK LACQUER BBQ SAUCE
Mix, jar and refrigerate:
>1/2 C. **hoisin sauce**
>3 tbsp. **orange marmalade**
>1 tsp. **instant coffee** dissolved in 1 tsp. hot **water**
>3 shakes of **cayenne pepper**.

FOODNOTES:
Great on ribs, roast duck and chicken. Add to baked beans for a zippy rendition of an old classic. Great for waking up last night's Chinese food. Keeps 2 months in the fridge.

GREENiES

TEQUILA LIME SALSA
Mix:
- 1/2 C. jarred **green salsa**, drained (you pick the heat)
- 1 1/2 tbsp. **lime juice**
- 3 tbsp. **olive oil**
- 2 tbsp. ready chopped **red** or **white onion**
- 2 tbsp. chopped fresh **cilantro**
- 1 tbsp. **Tequila** (optional)

Serve within 1 to 2 hours.

Great with grilled **shrimp**, **shrimp cocktail** (pg. 26), and seared **tuna**.
Pair with **blue** or **red** **tortilla chips** for a change.
Add to salads with 'Tex-Mex' flavors such as **Fajita Chop** (pg. 52) or
Heirloom Tomato Celebration. (pg. 54)

QUICKER NO LIQUOR
Just drain and measure the salsa. Add the **onions** and **cilantro** and
you're ready to go.

EMERALD SAUCE
Mix, jar, and serve:
- 1/2 C. **jalapeno jelly**
- 1/2 C. **mint jelly**
- 2 tbsp. **lime juice**
- 1/2 tsp. **wasabi mustard** (more **heat**? More **mustard**.)
- 2 tbsp. each, minced **cilantro** and **onion**
- 1 tbsp. minced fresh **mint**.

FOODNOTE:
This sauce is best served within 1-2 hours while the cilantro, green onions and
fresh mint are alive and crunchy. Store any remaining sauce in the fridge for a
week. Originally created for **Cream Cheese in a Hula Skirt** (pg. 16) and
One Cold Fish 2 Sauces (pg. 86). Makes a delicious sauce for lamb or fried
shrimp.

DECADENT DESSERT SAUCES

SULTRY CITRUS SAUCE
Mix, jar and refrigerate:
>1 C. orange **marmalade**, heavy on the rind
>2 tsp. fresh lime **zest**
>4 tbsp. fresh lime **juice**
>2 tbsp. **real maple syrup**
>1 tbsp. **Grand Marnier** or **Triple Sec** (optional)

Drizzle on fresh fruit for **Instant Tartlets** (pg. 116), toss with fruit for **Summer Pie** (pg. 118); a tasty and colorful splash on ice cream, sorbet, waffles, french toast and yogurt.

QUICKER, NO LIQUOR
1/2 C. **orange marmalade**
2 tbsp. **lime juice**
1 tsp. **lime zest**

SUPER SOUR SUGAR SYRUP
Microwave for 15-20 seconds to dissolve:
>1/2 C. **brown sugar**
>5 tbsp. lime **juice**

Add ready-glazed walnuts as garnish. (optional)

For **California Citrus Cake** (pg. 106) or hot **gingerbread**. Toss with cut **papaya**, **mangos** and **bananas** and top with shredded **coconut**.
A unique sweetener for **iced tea**.

NEW THOUGHTS ON A CHOCOLATE SAUCE
>1 C. *The Silver Palate's* **Very Fudge**, warmed.

Add any one or two of the five choices below:
- 1/4 C. **chopped unsalted walnuts** or **pecans**
- 1 tbsp. **candied ginger** and/or **dried cranberries**
- 1 tbsp. **mint** or **fruit liqueur** of your choice
- 2 tsp. **instant coffee** in 2 tsp. hot **water**
- **cayenne pepper** and **Chinese Five Spice** to taste

LOOKING BACK &
MOVING FORWARD

My food career has been very unconventional. No formal cooking lessons or culinary degrees, no 'sous-chefing' in restaurants; just an ever-constant love, curiosity and involvement with food.

LOOKING BACK

I grew up in **Cleveland, Ohio** in the 50's. I was a lucky little girl. Daddy would fly me to **New York** in his airplane, just to experience the Big City. While my mother pretended to hide her fears, I would wave "bye, bye" from the window of the Stinson as we took off.

We would stay at the **Savoy Plaza** before it was the General Motors building. We saw Broadway shows and ate at **Sardi's** and **Larre's**. I distinctly remember eating frog legs, snails, shad roe and skate wing. Even calf's brains with black butter and capers, which was like eating a pudding, only it tasted savory instead of sweet. Daddy ate them with gusto, so why not?

Food in Cleveland was an entirely different story. Only a few things worth mentioning: Fluffy, snow-white birthday cakes from **Hough Bakery**; shaved ham sandwiches at **Danny Budin's Deli**; dried lychee nuts from "Chinatown", which consisted of four restaurants on two short blocks in downtown Cleveland.

One of our forefathers of premium quality ready made cuisine, **Stouffers**, started out as a restaurant on Shaker Square. We all went there after dancing school. Best thing on the menu? The Mac 'n Cheese.

My mother was a very simple cook. Baked potatoes, baked apples…great steaks from Clyde the Butcher. Her roast duck was actually quite fabulous. Back then, "salad" meant iceberg lettuce and those cello-wrapped tomatoes, which were never red. They were like eating slices of soaked cardboard. I bet in those days you couldn't find any fresh basil or thyme in the whole city.

My father **Jack** was another story. He knew nothing about food except for what he liked. His curiosity was endless. With a twinkle in his eye, he visited Paris often, always wearing a beret. He spoke not a word of French yet between 'Café des Deux Magots' and 'La Brasserie de l'Isle St. Louis' he made himself understood by all.

After graduating from College I lived in **New York City**. I met **Martha Stewart** before she ever wrote her first book. She was a very successful stockbroker. Even then, I knew there was something very special about her. We became friends and when I moved to England she adopted my beautiful Persian cat, Magnolia.

I spent the early 70's working and living in **London**. The food halls at **Harrods** became my culinary mentor and friends began urging me to write down my recipes. My ongoing dilemma was that I loved to entertain yet never had any time. I became resourceful out of necessity.

MOVING FORWARD

I moved to Los Angeles in the late 70's. The supermarkets were growing more sophisticated. California cuisine was booming: **Spago**, **Michael's**, **Campanile**, **Zuni Cafe,** the pioneering **Alice Waters** with her amazing organic and sustainable food movement and of course, **Chez Panisse**. The vineyards of Northern California, were giving France a run for their Burgundy. It was a gastronomic explosion.

In 1980, my husband and I purchased a home in the **Ojai Valley**. Oranges and lemons grow as far as the eye can see. I learned how easily I could prepare elegant, simple meals with the use of fresh ingredients. Out of that inspiration, I created a line of citrus-based products and named it **The Ojai Cook**. That was in 1985. Today it is an award winning national brand of condiments and flavored mayonnaises.

I became a member of **NASFT** (National Association of Specialty Foods) and met others who were developing their own sophisticated products lines. We were at the dawn of a new era. Two decades later the availability of quality ready made products has increased tenfold. Specialty foods once unavailable to home cooks are now a click, a call or a short drive away.

Through the late 90's, I ran **The Ojai Cook Culinary Center**, a cooking school at the **Pacific Design Center** in Los Angeles. By then, my approach in the kitchen had boiled down to: "How can I make this taste extraordinary in the shortest amount of time?" Incorporating ready-prepared foods was the key to making shortcuts without sacrificing quality or flavor.

HERE
AND
NOW

Over the years I have come to love and rely upon my 'ready mades'. While America has grown obsessed with celebrity chefs, I reserve my praises for the unsung heroes of today's home kitchen. With this book I'd like to say "thank you" to the inventors of all these products. With their impeccable palates and a true gift for problem solving, these pioneers go the extra mile to develop their guarded recipes and innovations into convenient packages for our benefit.

I also tip my hat to today's sophisticated supermarkets for making quality prepared foods and ready made products readily available to the American public. I revel in the fact that I can pick up sushi, tabouli, pre-washed chopped veggies and a bunch of fresh herbs anytime I want, all in one stop.

Preparing fresh, great tasting meals at home does not need to be complicated or time-consuming. So...loosen up and get a little adventurous. Time to get a lot more intimate with your new best friend, the supermarket.

To novice and experienced cooks alike, here is my invitation to fall in love with food "assembly" and to embrace it as modern every day cuisine.

Joan Vogel

EATiNG
IS LIKE MAKING LOVE

PASSIONATE
INSTINCTIVE
TACTILE
INEXACT
EXPERIMENTAL
DELICIOUS
MESSY
SPONTANEOUS
EXHILARATING
DEMANDING
ESSENTIAL
HUMOROUS
REPETITIVE
CREATIVE
EUPHORIC

ACKNOWLEDGEMENTS

A verrrrry long and winding road this was. Full of discovery, frustration, encouragement, and amazing people. The concept of assembling sophisticated meals from prepared foods just wouldn't go away and I wanted to explore it further. Then there was luck and good timing.

My great friend **Stephanie Williams** introduced me to **Shelby Goodman**, a fabulously sophisticated woman who loves great food, and clever ideas. She loved the 'Quickies' concept.

She introduced me to a brilliant food stylist who also thought I had a unique perspective on home meal preparation for the 21st Century. Special thanks to him for believing in me from the beginning. **Norman Stewart** gave me his incredible talents of translating food into a real work of art.

He in turn introduced me to the brilliant and amazing **Jon Edwards**; professional food photographer extraordinaire. His genius makes you want to eat the pages. Without the generosity and talent of John Edwards and Norman Stewart this book would never be.

Thanks to **Heather Winters** for her quick and savy retouching skills.

The early visual team was world-renowned graphic designer **Keith Bright** and his group. Additionally, many many thanks to **May De Castro**, **Catherine Horrigan** and **Chelsea Ontiveros** for their style and visual panache.

But it was **Jonathan Licht** who really designed this book, with constant comments from me in the 'peanut butter gallery.'

Jonathan is amazing. He understood that zaniness and great design are not mutually exclusive; that the text and the visuals can laugh at each other and still be understood.

Big kisses to **Kim Chan**, who edited, tested, and kept me focused. I could not have finished "69 Quickies in the Kitchen" without her hours and hours of dedication, and her professional culinary skills. Many thanks as well to **Michelle Kramer** and **Nancy Mansfield** for testing and editing some assemblies.

As researchers, editors and publishing professionals I must thank: **Beverly Biggerstaff**, **Sarena Kirby**, **Michelle Vogel**, **Turon Vahedi**, **Lilla Hangay**, **Liz Camfiord**, **Martha Hopkins** and **Amy Treadwell**.

I can't forget my great friend **Louis Stern**, who said "Write the damn thing already," and encouraged me to put '69 Quickies' front and center on the cover.

My love and thanks to all who constantly cheered me on, my family and dear friends and any professionals whom I have forgotten.

SOME BRANDS WE LOVE

The following is an abbreviated list of the brands and companies that have inspired me to write this book. I could never remember all the culinary geniuses that I have met on my journey as 'The Ojai Cook' and 'The Shopping Cart Chef'.

All of these manufacturers, and more, have catapulted the American Supermarkets to be the best, most sophisticated, one-stop shopping places in the world. Their vision motivated by an ever increasing demand by an educated American public has given our world something far different than the choices of families in the 50's and 60's.

Congratulations to all those creative minds whose magic goes into bottles, boxes, freezers, snack packs in every corner of every store. An enormous Culinary Kiss to **THE NATIONAL ASSOCIATION FOR THE SPECIALTY FOOD TRADE, INC.** (NASFT) for bringing us all together so we can dazzle those retailers and consumers.

AL DENTE, INC.
WWW.ALDENTEPASTA.COM

B. R. COHN OLIVE OIL CO.
WWW.BRCOHNOLIVEOIL.COM

BAREFOOT CONTESSA PANTRY
WWW.STONEWALLKITCHEN.COM

BELLA CUCINA ARTFUL FOOD
WWW.BELLACUCINA.COM

BRENT & SAM'S COOKIES, INC.
WWW.BRENTANDSAMS.COM

BRIANNA'S FINE SALAD DRESSINGS
WWW.BRIANNASSALADDRESSING.COM

CABOT CREAMERY
WWW.CABOTCHEESE.COM

CHAR CRUST, INC.
WWW.CHARCRUST.COM

THE CHOCOLATE TRAVELER
WWW.THECHOCOLATETRAVELER.COM

CHRONICLE BOOKS
WWW.CHRONICLEBOOKS.COM

CIAO BELLA GELATO CO.
WWW.CIAOBELLAGELATO.COM

COACH FARM, INC.
WWW.COACHFARM.COM

CYPRUS GROVE CHEVRE
WWW.CYPRESSGROVECHEVRE.COM

DAVE'S GOURMET
WWW.DAVESGOURMET.COM

DIVINE PASTA CO.
WWW.DIVINEPASTA.COM

DUFOUR PASTRY KITCHENS, INC.
WWW.DUFOURPASTRYKITCHENS.COM

E. WALDO WARD & SON
WWW.WALDOWARD.COM

EL PASO CHILE CO
WWW.ELPASOCHILE.COM

GRAFTON VILLAGE CHEESE COMPANY
WWW.GRAFTONVILLAGECHEESE.COM

HINT MINT
WWW.HINTMINT.COM

J & M FOODS
WWW.JMFOODS.COM

JUST OFF MELROSE
WWW.JUSTOFFMELROSE.COM

KRINOS BRAND TARAMOSALATA
WWW.KRINOS.COM

LABREA BAKERY
WWW.LABREABAKERY.COM

LAURA CHENEL'S CHEVRE
WWW.LAURACHENEL.COM

JOHN WM MACY'S CHEESESTICKS
WWW.CHEESESTICKS.COM

MARCEL & HENRI
CHARCUTERIE FRANÇAISE
WWW.MARCELETHENRI.COM

MARIANI PACKING COMPANY
WWW.MARIANIFRUIT.COM

MCCONNELL'S ICE CREAM
WWW.MCCONNELLS.COM

MELISSA'S
WWW.MELISSAS.COM

MICHEL BLANCHET'S CORDON BLUE
WWW.MICHELCORDONBLEU.COM

NUESKE'S APPLEWOOD SMOKED MEATS
WWW.NUESKEMEATS.COM

N.Y. CAKE
WWW.NYCAKE.COM

THE OJAI COOK
WWW.QBFOODS.COM

PARTNERS CRACKERS
WWW.PARTNERSCRACKERS.COM

THE PERFECT BITE CO.
WWW.THEPERFECTBITECO.COM

PORT CHATHAM SMOKED SEAFOOD
WWW.PORTCHATHAM.COM

ROBERT ROTHSCHILD FARM
WWW.ROBERTROTHSCHILD.COM

RUBSCHLAGER BAKING CORP.
WWW.RUBSCHLAGERBAKING.COM

SARABETH'S KITCHEN
WWW.SARABETH.COM

SCHARFFENBERGER CHOCOLATE
WWW.SCHARFFENBERGER.COM

SILVER PALATE
WWW.SILVERPALATE.COM

ST. DALFOUR ET CIE.
WWW.STDALFOUR.COM

STONEWALL KITCHEN
WWW.STONEWALLKITCHEN.COM

T. MARZETTI CO.
WWW.MARZETTI.COM

LES TROIS PETITS COCHONS
WWW.3PIGS.COM

URBAN ACCENTS, INC.
WWW.URBANACCENTS.COM

URBANI TRUFFLES
WWW.URBANIT.COM

WALKERS SHORTBREAD
WWW.WALKERSSHORTBREAD.COM

iNDEX